© **Copyright 2023 - All rights reserved.**

You may not reproduce, duplicate or send the contents of this book without direct written permission from the author. You cannot hereby despite any circumstance blame the publisher or hold him or her to legal responsibility for any reparation, compensations, or monetary forfeiture owing to the information included herein, either in a direct or an indirect way.

Legal Notice: This book has copyright protection. You can use the book for personal purpose. You should not sell, use, alter, distribute, quote, take excerpts or paraphrase in part or whole the material contained in this book without obtaining the permission of the author first.

Disclaimer Notice: You must take note that the information in this document is for casual reading and entertainment purposes only. We have made every attempt to provide accurate, up to date and reliable information. We do not express or imply guarantees of any kind. The persons who read admit that the writer is not occupied in giving legal, financial, medical or other advice. We put this book content by sourcing various places.

Please consult a licensed professional before you try any techniques shown in this book. By going through this document, the book lover comes to an agreement that under no situation is the author accountable for any forfeiture, direct or indirect, which they may incur because of the use of material contained in this document, including, but not limited to, — errors, omissions, or inaccuracies

ONLINE DATING SUCCESS IN FIVE STEPS

CONTENTS

DISCLAIIMER NOTICE 3
WHAT YOU SHOULD KNOW BEFORE DATING ONLINE! 4
WHAT DIFFERS ONLINE DATING SO MUCH? 7
1 STEP : GETTING STARTED 16
STEP 2 : MAKING YOURSELF APPEAR LUXURIOUS 26
STEP 3 : ALLOWING YOUR RELASHIONSHIP TO GROW 39
STEP 4 : FACE-TO-FACE INTERACTION 45
STEP 5 : ONCE BITTEN 54

DISCLAIIMER NOTICE

Despite making every effort to be as precise and thorough as possible, the Publisher does not at any time guarantee or suggest that the contents of this report are correct due to the Internet's tendency to change quickly.

Although every effort has been taken to verify the content in this publication, the Publisher disclaims all liability for any mistakes, omissions, or other interpretations of the subject matter. Any perceived slights towards particular people, groups, or organizations are accidental.

Like everything else in life, there are no guarantees of income made in books with practical advice. Readers are advised to respond based on their own judgment regarding their own circumstances and take appropriate action.

This book is not meant to be a source for accounting, financial, legal, or business advice. All readers are urged to consult with qualified experts in the fields of law, business, accounting, and finance.

This book is recommended for printing for ease of reading.

WHAT YOU SHOULD KNOW BEFORE DATING ONLINE!

Before one delves into the complexities of online dating, there are many things that one must understand about it. It is not all fun and games. Although it may seem like the simplest thing in the world, online dating is not straightforward. It needs to be taken seriously, else, things can go out of hand. Every game has its own rules, and if you don't know them all, you'll never improve as a player or ultimately come out on top.

Tastes fluctuate

There are so many different types of individuals nearby. Just take a quick look about you. How many people do you recognize?
Sizes, builds, forms, and characteristics all vary greatly.

And that only deals with outward appearances. And the plot completely changes when it comes to the characters. Return to your former classrooms and have a peek around as you travel down memory lane.

One setting where we have the opportunity to connect closely with many different people is a classroom. We get to interact with a variety of people from quite varied backgrounds and get to know them personally. So how many of your peers did you really get along with?

Not as classmates, but as humans, is what I mean. Was it simple to get along with everyone? Because of this, we frequently have best friends or clichés in our classes.

We don't have to like everyone and we don't have to. While one person's tastes and interests may be completely at odds with ours, another person's tastes and interests may coincide with ours.

Therefore, the dating experience is mostly the same. However, there are conditions in place here. Unlike in a classroom setting, most people go on dates in order to find a life partner, which is a more remarkable goal. Before two individuals decide to spend the rest of their lives together, there are 101 things that need to be compatible.

Many people believe that they can handle dating on their own. They might be correct because no one is more familiar with a person's preferences than they are.

Perhaps the majority of us can choose without assistance, but wouldn't it be beneficial to learn a few tips on dating in general, especially online dating? This article was created with this goal in mind, so that the thousands of people who are currently using Internet dating can benefit the most from it.

Checking Out This eBook

I am aware that the majority of my readers lead very busy lives and don't have much time to read manuals.

I have therefore created something that may be understood with only a quick glance. To read this book cover to cover, you might need to set aside no more than 10 to 15 minutes. It's that easy. However, do not be fooled by the seeming simplicity. It is true that this effort is quite thorough and strives to cover every possible angle.

You can either use this book as a general how-to to expedite your match-hunting endeavor, or you can keep returning to it to double-check each step before you take it. There is absolutely nothing to be afraid of if you follow the advice in this book; you just won't fall.

WHAT DIFFERS ONLINE DATING SO MUCH?

We, as humans, have existed on this planet for tens of thousands of years. People have been selecting partners since before humankind began. People choose their life partners in a wide variety of ways since cultures around the world are so diverse.

But compared to the history of mankind as a whole, the idea of finding a life partner with the aid of the Internet is a relatively new one. It goes without saying that the Internet and computers have greatly impacted man's life, therefore it is not surprising that the Internet has become a factor in choosing a compatible spouse as well.

Simply described, online dating is the process of meeting a spouse online using a machine, specifically a computer. That alone makes the approach and concept extremely novel. Numerous happy individuals from all around the world have used online dating to discover compatible companions.

To be honest with you, though, a lot of unfortunate people have been duped and abandoned by the same procedure. So let's get into the specifics of online dating in order to ensure that you get a spot on the first list.

The Internet's Mysteries

Online dating is no different from the Internet in that regard. Because of the seemingly limitless communication options provided by the Internet, online dating has found this characteristic to be both a blessing and a curse.

Before the encounter, people can start over and learn everything there is to know about one another. Tastes and preferences, likes and dislikes, interests and obsessions can be shared privately so that the two parties are not at all strangers when the meeting actually occurs. Amazing, isn't it?

However, this potential for limitless communication also opens up a lot of room for deceit. The ability to use, abuse, and misuse the same object is a magnificent gift bestowed to the human species. Naturally, online dating has also been and continues to be utilized for despicable ends.

It could be a practical joker or someone with more sinister motives looking to prey on some unsuspecting victims who is abusing this resource. This is the reason why doing a little bit of homework is a smart idea before to leaving.

You do not, however, need to worry because the hard work has already been done for you. All you need to do is run your eyes over the lines below, and you will be ready to strike it rich.

Why Has Online Dating Grown To Be So Popular?

The cause is quite obvious. The same factors that made the Internet so well-liked also explain this phenomenon. A completely new world of interaction and communication is made possible via the Internet. And the following are the explanations for this.

Speed

Imagine what used to occur in the past when people had to rely on the reliable mail service. A person back then had to wait one or two days for a letter to reach someone who resided in the same state as them. It would take the second person one or two days to respond, and one or two days would pass before the first person received this letter.

Therefore, a single correspondence would actually last for a full week. But things have changed completely since then. Amazingly, the first letter and response were completed in only two minutes!

E-mail brings two people together more quickly than waiting, which may make the heart grow fonder.

Privacy The Internet also offers complete privacy. In the complete privacy of one's bedroom, bathroom, or any other location of one's choice, one can communicate with another person. Thanks to chat and e-mail features, there is no need to worry about being overheard or eavesdropped (yuck!).

Options and Possibilities

The only thing that the Internet lacks is actual contact, but it does offer other choices like voice chat and video conferencing. But who would want to initiate physical contact immediately early in a relationship?

Is there a better method to start a date where you can see the individual, speak to them, and hear their voice?

The economy

The Internet has made all of this and more possible, and the best part is that it costs you virtually nothing. A PC (who doesn't have one?) and an Internet connection (how can anyone live without one?) are all that are required. and you are ready to go. The only thing you could want is a step-by-step manual on how to select your ideal date, and you can get that right here!

So why are we still waiting?

Be Specific With Your Goals

Man is, as we all know, a social being. But the human being is also a lonely one. (And by "guy," we also mean women.) Man craves companionship.

Not only from friends and family, but also from that particular someone with whom he or she can share those sweet nothings, those everyday joys and sorrows, someone with whom they may start a whole new life together and raise their own family.

Finding a life partner is now a basic need of man. And dating is the most often utilized technique for this. Please keep in mind that when we talk about dating in the truest sense of the word, it is not to be considered as a step toward sleeping together. Much more than that is involved. It is the first stage in selecting a life companion, and internet dating has now greatly streamlined the procedure.

Choosing a Casual Relationship over Marriage

Your actions and desires are fully up to you at this point. I don't want to sound nosey but I would like to draw a fine line between the kind of dating that is involved in these two quests.

Of course we are all grown up and so let us act like grown ups. Obviously in a casual relationship we are looking for fun. And mind you, fun can have a lot of connotations. So here the object of one's desire will obviously be a person who is not inclined towards a serious relationship.

If both parties are of the same view then it is well and good because they understand each other perfectly and do not expect much from such a relationship. This leaves no room for heartbreak.

It is when one party is in for something more serious and the other party is into sheer frivolousness that the problems start. So you should be absolutely clear about what you are looking for from the start, and you should make your intentions very clear to the other person.

At the same time you should have no doubts about the intentions of the other person as well. Remember, even if it is a casual relationship, there should be mutual understanding at least about the nature of the relationship.

Of course, there is yet another possibility where a casual relationship can blossom into something more serious. But, again in such cases it is your instincts that can help you identify what is good and what is bad.

No matter how strong a person is, anyone can be taken for a ride or be taken for granted. Being jilted is never a nice experience. So those of you who are going in for a casual relationship, for heavens sake, be on your guard! Marriage is altogether a different story but we will deal with that later.

Dating Comes From a Fundamental Need

Let's face it, of course sex is important, but sex is by far NOT the most important reason for dating.

Important! Maybe during the age of thoughtless youth, when new hormones are being pumped in and out, sex is on every one's mind. But as one matures (mind you that does not mean growing old and gray) sex takes the back seat and mutual support, likes and dislikes, cooperation, caring and sharing come to the forefront. We start thinking about building up a world of our own and we need someone to share it with, and not just someone to sleep with.

Sex is a fundamental need of every human being. We all have it in us to give and receive physical pleasure. But when you sit and think about it for a minute, you can see that this urge is actually the result of another urge.

There is a more primary urge in every human being to breed and produce offspring, and it is this urge that gives rise to such a powerful sexual desire. But whatever be the urge, the most dignified means to satisfy it is dating.

Nobody, not one of us, is complete without a partner; and it is to satisfy this need that people date. Because of this, the rest of this manual will be dedicated not to finding the right sex partner, but to finding the right life partner.

Online Dating Is Here To Stay

Let's accept the fact that dating couldn't really get better. Online dating is THE real thing. Let's compare it to the old system of evening balls or social gatherings. Imagine you are this big gathering where there are a lot of men and women looking out for suitable partners.

Suppose you bump into one or two people with whom you seem to strike an immediate rapport. You are then able to take this person out onto a balcony with just the moon to keep an eye on you.

You get to talk to this person for hours and hours; just talk and nothing else. You get to discuss likes and dislikes and finally when it is time to part you leave with a promise to meet on a following day at an equally enjoyable spot. These talks go on for days and weeks and finally you decide that this indeed is the THE person with whom you want to spend the rest of your life with.

Then of course you start meeting in more open places, you hold hands and even kiss. You begin to go out for lunch and dinner and spend even more intimate time together. When the moment is right and your decision is made, it then becomes time for you to say, "I do."

Sigh! It sounds like a nice fairy tale, doesn't it?

Well it needn't be. It could be your own love story because the concept of online dating is just what has been described above. If you click the right buttons everything could work out fine for you and we have evidence to prove it. Just take a look at the figures given below and you can behold for yourself what a universal phenomenon online dating has already become.

As I mentioned earlier, one of the best things about online dating is that it affords a lot of privacy. You can chat for hours, video conference, or do whatever it is you care to do without arousing the interest of others or attracting the wrong kind of attention. All you need is a computer and Internet access everything becomes as discreet as can be. But along with that, may I add that we need a little bit of common sense as well or else we might find ourselves within the clutches of many lurid monsters lurking out there.

Another good thing about online dating is that it saves a lot of money which otherwise you would have had to splurge each time you took someone out on a date. It is because of these reasons and many more personal reasons that thousands of people find online dating to be a great convenience.

How To Get The Most Out Of Online Dating

Many people who decide to give online dating a try often end up with their hair singed and fingers burnt.

The reason we decided to put together such a manual is that online dating is not as simple as it looks. You need to know how to go about it in order to get the best out of it. Most people do not like to take chances and when it comes to finding a life partner people do not want to take chances at all.

But you can relax for through this manual we will be dealing with all the do's and the don'ts and so the whole process will be quite easy and enjoyable to you. This manual will provide you with step-by-step instructions on how to being online dating.

We have no doubts about the decision-making abilities of our readers and so we do not propose to give a lot of advice on the issue. Our purpose is simply to provide a couple of guidelines which we hope our readers will find valuable as they proceed in the attempt to find the perfect partner.

1 STEP : GETTING STARTED

Angels will not walk where fools enter hastily.

Always proceed cautiously when entering uncharted territory. Before really going out there and starting to deal your cards, you need to make a plan. Be confident in yourself and in your desires. In a chat room, anybody and everyone is free to type whatever they want, but that doesn't mean we have to follow suit.

Everyone can access the Internet, which is a good feature. However, this same quality draws all different types of people to it. However, just because a number of users in a chat room have nothing but trash on their minds, doesn't mean that everyone else is the same. You can obtain the proper kind of response if you remain composed and retain your composure.

Internet users can range from the nice to the rude, depending on what you do. The golden rule is applicable here: treat others as you would like them to treat you. The game has no established rules. Everybody is a player. However, you are not required to act like a rogue simply because others do. Your strategy is the only thing that will enable you to receive the desired response.

It doesn't seem very sane to me to decide all of a sudden that you want to use the internet to find a date. You are essentially putting yourself up for sale if you simply enter a chat room and declare that you are available; you are unlikely to receive the outcomes you are hoping for.

We must all be aware of the fact that everyone in a chat room is on an equal footing. Don't believe the myth that joining a chat room is like strolling into a ballroom wearing your best. The most eligible person—read that as the sexiest person of the other sex—then notices you and moves closer to you as everyone turns to look at you.

We all know that only in James Bond movies can things like that occur, and Bond himself never enters into committed relationships. For him, everything is a game.

Where Should You Begin?

The first piece of advice we have for you is to refrain from immediately entering a chat room for singles in search of a potential match. Each of us is aware that the majority of these chat rooms are practically overrun with individuals who are primarily interested in having sex. This means that anything you ask for will always result in that, defeating the goal. You'll never meet someone whose hobbies and preferences are somewhat similar to yours.

It can occasionally get incredibly irritable. It everything gets off to a good start. The subject suddenly shifts to the three-letter word when you are enjoying a pleasant chat and getting to know someone. You sigh and have the choice of blocking that individual's communications or running the danger of that person criticizing you in a public chat room. Normally, you are required to quit the chat room entirely.

In other words, getting someone to sleep with you is the easy part; however, if you're searching for something more lasting, such as a life partner, you'll need to be a little more patient. Finding the best of the lot is difficult. It will be worthwhile if you do discover it, though.

So, instead of entering a singles' chat room, you could try approaching the situation from a different perspective. Consider trying to proceed backward.

Besides Appearances

Try to sit for a minute or two and consider the things that interest you and the qualities that you would want to see in a person.

I don't mean things in the physical sense when I say "things" here. I'm not talking about something that you would find interesting about someone's physical appearance. Once more, a line must be drawn between a serious relationship and a casual one. The value of the physical characteristics is always paramount in casual relationships. What a person looks like and what they have been given are more important to us.

On the other side, if we have a serious connection, physical characteristics are less significant. The most crucial element in this case is certainly compatibility. Along with that, there are some characteristics that we will undoubtedly be on the lookout for. We're discussing mental attributes here. Beauty is merely superficial, after all!

Although this notion can seem weird, it is true. The premise is that a person's appearance is something that can be grown to like. As soon as you like the person's personality, you'll begin to like them overall. Even if a person doesn't have the appearance of a Hollywood celebrity, it is still totally feasible to fall in love with them. One of nature's tricks is to do that.

Many people insist on viewing the other person's photo first before formally committing to a relationship. Of course, they may have their reasons, but I for one believe that a choice like this, made mostly solely on appearances, is better suited for a casual relationship. After a while, it will inevitably cool off. After all, how long can you hold someone's gaze? And what happens if they don't return your gaze?

What if, even worse, you catch the person glancing intently at someone else? Even though appearances can be essential, they are by no means the most crucial aspect of a relationship and should never be the determining factor.

Shared Interests

A person is not comparable to a piece of glass through which you can peer to see the other side. Humans are more like diamonds, which when held up to light reflect and deflect light such that a variety of hues may be seen. We're complicated.

There are many different interests among us, thus it is not necessary for one person's interests to coincide with another's. But happily, there are fewer interests than people. So there will undoubtedly be many people who are interested in the same things as us. And our search should be over if we can locate someone who fits that description. So, what do you find interesting? You need to learn that, after all.

However, before you scale back your choices, you might need to give it some serious thought. You may like doing a number of things, but you may not have given them much thought.

It's possible that sports or outdoor activities are among your hobbies. You could also consider hobbies like crossword puzzles, social work, or religion. Please remember that the words I've provided here are merely recommendations and to keep the ball moving.

Your preferences and interests could be very dissimilar. So leave them to it. Choosing your interests is the first step in finishing the story.

What About A Person Interests You?

Most likely, this is the story's most significant development. Each of us needs to take a seat and consider what we want in a partner. Similar interests do not guarantee that you will get along with someone.

For instance, just because you enjoy talking a lot doesn't necessarily guarantee that you will get along with someone else who enjoys talking a lot. There can't be a conversation if two individuals try to talk at the same time, of course.

Additionally, there won't be much conversation if both of you are quiet and restrained. "Compatible" is the word used here. Partners' objectives should not conflict and should instead complement one another.

Term searches

Try such keyword searches on a search engine like Google now that you've identified what it is about a person that attracts you as well as what your hobbies and preferences are.

Not promoting oneself as someone looking for a life partner is the goal here. No matter how skillfully you phrase it, it loses its delicacy the moment you enter a chat room for singles. Therefore, refrain from carrying out that action in that manner. You may recall our discussion about working backwards; this is how it is done.

In a subsequent chapter, we will discuss how to present yourself in the best possible light, but for the time being, let's talk about meeting Mr. or Mrs. Right. It's noteworthy to notice that falling in love or making a decision is not a difficult process in this situation. Making the proper decision and finding the perfect person to fall in love with is the challenging part.

Favorite Things vs.

Making a list of traits in people who you actually detest is the second thing you could do. And no, I'm not joking. Likes are crucial, but dislikes may even be more significant. We all have to make a few adjustments here and there, but if we start out by tolerating behaviors that we actually detest, it will eventually have an impact on the relationship.

I'd want to issue a warning in this area. When they are courting, many people make mistakes. They put up their finest act, which is obviously quite good, but they also attempt to be very accommodating, which is not very nice. The fact that they will be spending the rest of their life with the person they are trying to impress rather than just going on a camping vacation with them is something that they frequently overlook.

Therefore, it is best to refrain from being "oh so very accommodating and adjusting."

You have the money to stick to your guns when it comes to some matters. Furthermore, forget about trying to change the offender's bad habits down the road.

Whatever the behavior, the instant you start attempting to change it or coax it out of the person, the word becomes "nagging," and if the person ever does stop doing it, they will dislike you less for it.

Really, it doesn't operate that that. It is therefore best to be aware of the traits and behaviors that you truly detest in others and to avoid 'lesser mortals' who possess those traits and behaviors.

You will be in a better position to make the best decision after you have a fairly clear notion of your preferences. And because there are so many people, you don't need to fret or be overly concerned that you might not find someone at all. He or she is out there, and you will succeed if you do what you are doing correctly, which is to bark up the appropriate tree.

Some people even hold the view that everything is predetermined. Who should wed whom has been predetermined, and only that which is predetermined will ultimately occur. I'm not sure about that, but I do know that dating makes the process go more quickly.

Alternatively, you may just stand by and allow nature to run its course. Oh, the great things about nature. The choice of a mate involves a lot of chemistry, so perhaps it would be better if we let nature to handle the process on her own.

Initial Friends

Consider this as an effort to make many friends—good friends, I mean—rather than as a search for a future spouse or partner. Friends who can make you laugh out loud and are funny themselves. Not everyone has the ability to make us laugh, and when I say laugh, I don't mean from a comic. Here, we're discussing friends.

Having a large social network is beneficial. One's life is made richer by it. With friends, you can be who you are, which is the best thing. They can be authentic with you as well. That necessitates letting everything out. We must always keep in mind that a spouse should not only be a faithful partner, but also a best friend.

One error that most couples make is this one. They frequently view their friends and spouses as two separate entities. While having your own pals is totally OK, your spouse or partner should always be your best friend.

It should be someone you can talk to about your hopes and anxieties, who you can confide in, who has empathy, who can hold your hand when things go wrong, and who can bring joy to even the darkest of days.

All of this is obviously extremely different from having sex. We did emphasize before that choosing a life partner should be based on more important factors than appearance and sexual attraction. The marriage proposal must follow a natural progression; it should not, however, be the first thing that comes to mind as you get to know someone. Saying something like, "Hey, you know what, I think we have the same preferences so let's get married," is simply not acceptable.

Yes, you can say that, but it would not be in good taste. So what do you do if you find out that one of your new friends—the one you were crossing your fingers would become engaged—is already married?

Have you have a car? The solution is then straightforward—you just run over that person's spouse and get rid of the undesirable component, right? Wrong! Just simply not done. You can still be friendly with that individual while focusing on something else. Who knows, you might even come across a better individual. You just need to deal the cards again after shuffling them.

I believe you now understand what we meant when we said we were working backwards. Good. There is also another catch to this method. There's a possibility that one of the friends you met read this book as well, and the proposal could come from the other side.

If so, that's great since you won't have to perform the ceremony.

Mr. and Mrs. Right and Wrong

But what if the person making the proposal wasn't actually who you had in mind? Of course, the decision is yours to make; you are free to accept or reject it. But there is something here that is worth thinking about. It's great if we can find someone we love, but isn't it wonderful if we can find someone who also loves us?

However, I also want to add a word over here. What if someone were to approach you and make a proposal, but you would sadly have zero interest? Although you have every right to decline the offer, kindly do so politely. It's not necessary to insult the other person's ego. Your friendship with this person makes it clear that you value them greatly. A declined proposal, however, is preferable to a divorce if you are aware that you cannot wed this individual.

Try to be as compassionate as you can when expressing your emotions.

STEP 2 : MAKING YOURSELF APPEAR LUXURIOUS

Nobody in this world is perfect, but that does not mean we cannot strive to look our best. Giving nature a helping hand is completely acceptable. Improve your appearance, profile, and brand by working on all three.

This is me; whether you like it or not, it's your problem, is a common way of thinking. I won't alter my ways. Nobody is asking you to change, so what are you actually attempting to do? scare off visitors?

The truth is that such words are only an expression of your own insecurities. Everyone experiences insecurity to some extent, perhaps some more so than others. This uncertainty is what makes us come out as stern and insensitive when it comes to enhancing our appearances.

Please tell me what you're terrified of. You have a tip from me. Everyone is terrified of the same things that you are. Most people in this world do not support or oppose us. They are considering themselves.

It takes a lot of effort to present oneself, but oddly, this is the area that individuals most frequently overlook. The majority of us approach describing ourselves with a relaxed attitude. We have a lot of work to do when it comes to how you present yourself.

If we had known you better on a personal level, we would have loved to assist you in creating a profile of yourself that was as stunning as possible. Of course, it is not possible to get to know each and every one of our readers individually.

However, you need not be concerned because we have done extensive research in this area and, if you follow our recommendations, you may create the profile of your dreams.

Describe Your Dream

Making a profile cannot require too much time or effort. It is a matter that demands complete seriousness. Please don't take this matter lightly. Wouldn't you spend a lot of time getting your résumé ready if you were applying for a job?

Well, the majority of us work for four or five years on average. And what about relationships? Definitely, we do not get into relationships with the hope that they will only endure a few years.

Since choosing a partner is perhaps the most significant choice you will ever make in your life, we must realize that relationships are actually worth much more than jobs. Let's now talk about how you may improve your profile.

Of course, you can hire a professional to complete the task since it would save you time and work. Of course, there may be a tiny cost involved, but it might be worthwhile. A photo on the profile is something that many people are reluctant to do. I won't press the matter, I suppose. Although it does appear better to include a picture in your profile, you might choose not to do so because of privacy concerns.

The best thing you could do is send your image over as an attachment or a file after you are confident that this person is not lying to you and you feel comfortable conversing with them. However, it is advisable to do this on a reciprocal basis as well. If you are aware of someone else's appearance but they are not, and vice versa, it would be unjust.

The Person Reflected

Now that we are talking about the photograph, please send a good-quality photo if you are sending one of yourself. Please do not compromise on the quality, and it should be a recent photo. Hire an expert to complete the task for you; thanks to modern digital technology, they will likely produce excellent results.

Work on your expression concurrently before the picture is shot. To choose the expression you think suits you the best, stand in front of the mirror and experiment with different ones. Remember that you must be smiling in the photo as well. The "butter-will-not-melt-in-my-mouth expression" and the traditional hang dog expression are inappropriate. Smiling is free and it brightens people's faces significantly.

The first thing you should do is get a pen and paper and start writing down as many basic facts about yourself as you can. When we say "raw details," we mean stuff like your age, height, and weight.

We're going to work on this as the framework. And after we have given this backbone enough flesh and blood, even you will be impressed by your profile! However, let's avoid several pitfalls that the majority of people make first.

Modesty's Death Trap

Most of us were taught to be extremely modest. Speaking highly of ourselves makes us quite uneasy, even when it is in our best interests. Correct, nobody is asking you to blow the trumpet, but facts must be conveyed as such.

If you enjoy music and have a nice voice, I don't see why you couldn't record it that way. Why can't you just say, without seeming overly boastful, that you have a nice voice? Consider adding something like, "My friends think that I sing fairly well," as a tip to keep in mind.

There, you can't really feel bad about something that straightforward. The equivalent would be to remark, "Some people think I sing well, but it's up to you to judge whether I have a decent voice or not." The following are similar statements that you can edit and possibly add to.

"A lot of people like my cooking,"

"I'm no Rembrandt, but I like to paint,"

"I like to decorate, and a lot of my friends say my style isn't too bad."

So go ahead, if you really are great, you might as well let people know about it. After all, someone who is talented would always like to have a partner who appreciates them.

I want to address a specific query right now while we are discussing modesty. It's something that we're all familiar with. The question must have come up before if you've engaged in conversation with someone you're attempting to get to know better. What do you look like, is the query.

The purpose of this inquiry has frequently baffled me. My greatest responses were, "I resemble a hybrid between an ape and a Tasmanian devil," or "I have my mother's teeth, my father's nose, my uncle's eyes, and my roommates' shoes."

We cannot, however, respond in such a way that, amusing as they may be, might irritate the person. Is it really "are you well looking or not?" that they mean?

Definitely a challenging question! How can you respond to such a question without coming across as overly modest or overly vain? Not giving them the solution straight away is the best course of action. You might remark, "I am as fresh as peppermint," for example.

I resemble a cluster of new lilies, someone once said.

"I appeal like a bowl of fresh fruit,"

Give a thorough description of every inch if the person is still refusing to get the clue before letting them make their own decision.

pitfalls of the braggart

As we all know, boasting is really unappealing. It is therefore advisable to fully avoid it. This is especially true when it comes to physical characteristics. Even if you may have a great sense of style, let the other person make the final decision. Keep in mind that what is wine to Peter may be venom to Paul.

You can imply things like "I'm not ugly," "opinions are split; some people believe I'm good-looking, while others don't," or "I'm not a bad-looker, either." But perhaps adding a little comedy to it would be the greatest way to describe yourself.

I am round in all the appropriate areas, I hope, you may say if you're overweight. You may say something like, "Some say I should play basketball," if you are tall. You may say something along the lines of "I might look to lacking in size but I assure you, it is all there" if you are on the shorter side.

You know what the nicest part of making such amusing self-referential remarks is? Fun is always effective. We all possess a sense of humor, at least to some extent, and the ability to make humorous remarks about oneself is always attractive. And I'll tell you right now that humor makes like a billion bucks in sales.

The Clichéd Pitfall

These kinds of self-descriptions sort of sink into our heads because we have seen and heard other people use them. When someone asks us to describe ourselves, we immediately use such cliched language.

I believe it is far better to avoid using clichés at all costs. We appear to be simply another name in the crowd as a result. Do you know someone who looks precisely like you, unless you have an identical twin?

Then why in the world does your self-description seem like a repetitive piece of banal music? As much as you can, try to sound original. Make sure you sound intriguing.

Make an effort to compare and simile as much as you can. Don't just declare you're blonde if you are, though. You might say something like, "My hair is the color of newly cut hay."

You could say, if you are a brunette, "My hair color would make a raven blush." You may say, "My hair is like the setting sun," if you have red hair.

You do not need to minimize yourself, I would like to add as a second point. It all depends on how you look at it, but every coin has two sides. There is no justification, for instance, to feel self-conscious about having dark skin. It all relies on how you communicate it. You might use phrases like "If you enjoy chocolate then you are going to love the color of my skin," to get the desired effect. Alternately, "My body resembles polished wood."

Keep in mind that beauty is subjective, thus it is up to you to persuade the beholder. If you can convince people enough, the majority of people will believe what you say.

The Danger of Boredom

Make sure you sound as intriguing as you possibly can. I'm serious. Use the appropriate colors if you're painting a portrait of yourself. What do we do just before leaving home? In an effort to look as presentable and impressive as possible, we all spend at least five minutes in front of our mirrors.

The same holds true for our profile. Take out any dull details about you that the reader could find uninteresting. Simply state that you are an editor if your employment involves, for example, editing journals on the etymology of words derived from ancient Aramaic.

Likewise, make an effort to keep in mind that anything can be said in two different ways. Work on it till you are confident that it won't bore a reader to death. The easiest way to test this is to give it to a close friend and ask for that friend's opinion. Make every effort to avoid sounding monotonous because no one likes a bore.

The Pitfall of Vagueness

However, nothing you write about yourself should be ambiguous. The sentence "although I am not really given to sports, nor am I thought to be an outdoor person, I have developed a passing interest in watching football, and have had my periods with Terra firma" just does not cut it.

Phew! Statements like these undoubtedly repel people if anything. Avoid sayings like "I am different," especially when discussing your appearance, for the love of God. The other individual will very certainly visualize a lion-tailed monkey or a three-horned monster.

Using the expressions "I don't play by the rules" or "I am game for something new" is another example. These expressions can be utterly deceptive, and adding a sexual implication is the simplest thing in the world to do. Doing so will guarantee that you bite off more than you can chew.

Let's go on to the actual profile now that we've covered the primary issues. The fact that the profile needs to accurately represent who you are is why I said "genuine profile."

The Deceitful Web

It is best to avoid lying, even if you take considerable care to hide your identity.

Avoid trying to lie your way through a relationship because eventually it might all come out, and as we all know, one lie leads to another until the relationship as a whole falls apart. While taking care to keep your identity a secret, be as truthful and honest as you can.

Someone once stated that a friend is someone who knows everything about you and yet loves you. So there's no reason to keep anything about you hidden. Naturally, you do not have to divulge every horrifying, graphic detail about yourself to the person, but you also do not have to make up information about yourself that is just untrue.

If you ever portray a really positive image of oneself, including things that are simply untrue or are fantastical exaggerations, and the other person decides to change their mind for you, you will actually be basking in their success. You simply do not fit the picture that you have painted.

Your False Self

You must be astute while deciding on a handle to use to identify yourself. Don't try to woo as many partners as you can. After all, which do we value more, quantity or quality? Make an effort to only draw in those you find fascinating and who would find you engaging.

That's why we advised you to choose a handle that more accurately reflects who you are as a person. Avoid attempting to sound like a sex god or goddess. If you are, allow the other person to make that decision for yourself (rather than having them ask, "Is it in yet?"). Therefore, stay away from handles like "Megastud," "Handsomehunk," "Superbabe," or "Bedlover."

You may try handles that would give them a better understanding of who you are instead. Use Natureguy or Naturegirl if you enjoy the outdoors; Musicman or Musicmaid if you are a music enthusiast. If you enjoy theater and related activities, you might choose a name like Theaterguy or Theatergirl.

Gaining the favor of those with similar interests to your own is the goal. Naturally, this enhances the likelihood that you will click with the person.

Aim for Briefness

Being as succinct as you can while writing your profile is another important consideration. Nobody, and I mean nobody, wants to go through endless pages of someone else's profile. If you make it too wordy, the person reading it will assume you are the type of person who loves to talk endlessly about themselves and would rather for the reader to curl up and die rather than go on a date with you.

That doesn't mean, though, that you have to keep the entire essay to a few words. A profile that is too short could give the impression that you are doing this out of curiosity because you don't have the time.

Being completely natural would be the finest approach you could take. As you would while introducing yourself to a person in person, write your profile. The conversational approach, I should say, has the most appeal. Keep it straightforward and avoid using flowery language and clichés.

Authentic You

Take a moment to consider it. In the mirror, observe your own face. Do you resemble anyone else you know? Although we all share the same exterior features—one nose, one mouth, two eyes, and two ears—we all have incredibly distinct appearances.

In light of the fact that we have the same structural components, why must we sound the same when we can appear so different? Change the way you view yourself. When developing your profile, take into account more than simply your likes and dislikes. Think about your best traits. What exactly are attractive qualities?

These are the traits that make people like you. These are things that, of course, we never think about, but perhaps we should. So my advice would be to find out the reason your best pals like you. Who knows, their responses might pleasantly surprise you! But at least you'll have a general concept of what to put in your profile.

To determine what kind of person you are, undertake the following activity. The results might be fascinating, however I won't say they are 100% foolproof.

Animal experiment

Which of the following creatures most closely resembles you?

The shark

If you picked a shark, you tend to be an aggressive type of person who has no patience for others who are not up to par. The other options are: a rabbit, a bear, a hen, a dog, and finally a cat. When someone gets in your way, you won't hesitate to cut them down since you know exactly what you want and how to achieve it.

If you picked a rabbit, you tend to be cautious but sweet-tempered. You bend with great ease. You like to avoid the spotlight whenever possible and do not meddle too much in other people's business.

If you picked the bear, you are a warm person by nature but unsure about whether other people will like you. As a result, you could go out of your way to make friends and genuinely enjoy comforting others.

If you selected the hen, you belong to the group of people who are always fussing over trivial matters. Although you are highly dependable and always keep an eye out, occasionally you could find yourself interfering with matters that are unimportant to you.

If you choose the dog, you are a positive, upbeat person. You are willing to assist others, but if you don't exercise caution, you could occasionally end up being duped. You don't worry about little things, but when your head is lost, it really is lost.

You chose the cat, didn't you? You obviously live in your own world; you don't bother anyone else and don't enjoy being bothered by others. You are, in essence, the modern apartment creature that is aware of all manners but only employs them when necessary to be polite.

Although the descriptions provided here are merely broad recommendations, I believe they can serve as inspiration for your own profile. By yourself, you can accomplish it. Think about your favorite bird or animal. Think on aspects or characteristics that you enjoy rather than physical characteristics.

Then, sit down and quickly write a description of the animal, and voila! Before you know it, your profile is complete, however it would be a good idea to remove the animal's name before posting it.

I want every reader to comprehend a certain concept. We all have a unique quality that makes us stand out. Finding out what those characteristics are is the only thing left to do. Do not always take what others say about you at face value. You should talk about yourself, don't you?

As though you were speaking to your best buddy, pretend. Chat with yourself. Wouldn't you be ready to reassure someone if their best friend were to ask you what their best traits are? So, you are also affected by the same issue. Being your own best buddy is possible. Additionally, you are prepared with a list of your strengths when you do this activity on yourself. Common sense dictates that if you can do something to your friend, you can certainly do it to yourself.

Such a task is highly beneficial not only in terms of dating, but also in terms of understanding the type of person we deserve to meet. Only when we are aware of our strengths can we know what kind of partner we should look for. The same is true of our flaws, yet nobody is perfect, so nobody is perfect.

STEP 3 : ALLOWING YOUR RELASHIONSHIP TO GROW

We've listed our profiles, listed our interests, and are as prepared as we can be. The image is flawless. Nearly feeling alone at this upscale restaurant, looking stunning, holding a glass of champagne in one hand and the chair's back with the other. You're inviting with a smile on your lips, a twinkle in your eye, and a twinkle in your eye.

What happens next, then? This person, who seems to be the ideal fit for you, attracts your attention and strolls over to you. What will you now do? Keep in mind that the description above was of a virtual world. In essence, what we meant to say was that this is the mood you are going to create when spending time idly in a chat room.

What happens next if someone follows the cue and starts talking? That is a very thoughtful question, to be sure. I want to make one thing clear over here. Comparable to any other roadway is the Internet. Before you become familiar with your surroundings, it is not safe. Therefore, my advice would be to follow your gut and exercise caution. Despite the fact that you might come off as a really friendly person, please use utmost caution while disclosing any personal information.

Pet names and Nicknames

Tell the other person that you prefer to be addressed by the handle you use, or even better, ask them to call you by your pet name, but make it clear that this is a pet name. This is because, if the relationship ends up being long-lasting, it won't be attractive to have to explain later that your real name is Heptullah and that you were just lying to you.

The greatest course of action in this situation would be to let people know you by a famous name. You might go by the names Veronica, Betty, Archie, Pocahontas, Cinderella, or Betty. It's time to start conversing and exchanging information. Stay away from the details and stick to the broad concepts.

Increasing Memory

Indeed, the human brain is an amazing organ. Even a supercomputer would be intimidated by it when compared to its capacity for storing and processing a vast variety of data. Our memories, however, have gotten much more selective as a result of the virtual information explosion.

As a result, we are unable to remember everything that we hear or see. When it comes to online conversations, do not place too much reliance in your recollection. There are many people you might encounter online, and you might communicate with a few of them. Therefore, with time, it may be challenging to recall each of them, along with their specifics.

Or even worse than that, you might become disoriented and conflate different details. If you address someone incorrectly or inquire about their personal information, it will reflect poorly on you. If you find yourself in a situation where you have been conversing with several people, for goodness sake write down each person's information separately or make different files for each person and store them on your computer.

Use names or handles that will make it easier for you to remember them when you start speaking with them later on when you add them to your friends list.

Playing the guessing game is not a good idea if you don't actually remember the person. If you say something like, "Is it Sarah or Mary?" the other person can become really insulted.

The best course of action in such circumstances is to be upfront with the person and say, "I know we spoke the other day, but I'm extremely sorry, can you kindly refresh my memory about you?"

Small Talk

There are a select few themes that work best for first-time conversations in order to avoid intimacy while also avoiding the need to search for topics of interest. The environment, sports, movies, music, and even food are all fair game.

However, it is also inappropriate to bring up family issues, politics, or religion right away. However, dirty jokes should be avoided, at least during the first few conversations.

Remember that this is the first step towards virtual intimacy, so you must trust your instincts and nothing else. Once you have spoken to someone more than once or twice and you feel comfortable with them, you can offer them your email address. This moves information out of the open chat rooms and into the personal inboxes.

Avoid Instant Intimacy

Many individuals believe that emails will never possess the warmth or the personal touch of the traditional letters and cards that people used to send via the postal service. That might be the case, but email has the benefit of being available immediately.

Because you are aware that the person with whom you are conversing is attempting to connect with you in a similar manner to how you are attempting to connect with them, there is a propensity for an intimacy to develop even before you realize it.

When someone pressures you for information that you must provide right away, the medium ceases to be the determining factor, and unless you are well-prepared, you may let certain data slip out.

The person you are conversing with is, after all, a stranger and goodness-knows-what, so you have to be constantly vigilant and keep reminding yourself of this. Avoiding immediate intimacy entirely is the best course of action.

It doesn't really matter if the other person thinks you're distant or chilly; you can simply fix that by explaining that it takes time for you to get up to someone. It's better to say, "Well, I'm sorry, I'm not the loose kind who plays about," than to have that trait, which is actually a good attribute.

Many of my readers might be interested to learn how to determine whether the other person is telling the truth. We must be very certain of the other person's good intentions before disclosing any personal information about ourselves on the Internet, as I had previously warned you. Therefore, that is the whole focus of the following section.

Four techniques for spotting lies We won't use singles chat rooms that are only for online dating, as was already said. We'll be in special interest discussion groups instead. Therefore, probing very specific questions about the subject of interest with a person is a very efficient technique to determine whether they are telling the truth. You should avoid wasting your time on someone who stumbles or delivers evasive responses.

Another thing you may do is to record any information the person decides to provide with you right away. Then, when you see them again, casually inquire about those facts; if there is a discrepancy between the two, you can be absolutely certain that they are lying.

Ask the person questions that may appear generic, but which should actually have a very specific purpose. For instance, you might inquire about what the person is seeking in a connection of this sort. Take note of the response. Ask the same question again after two or three encounters to see if the two responses agree.

You may attempt to act as though you have spoken with the person previously and naively inquire as to whether he or she is such and such a person (make something up). You could also attempt to flatter the person by saying something like, "I really enjoyed speaking with you the other day. You were absolutely pleasant, and so forth. It is evident that the person makes it a hobby to communicate with people using different identities if they fall for such cheap flattery.

The conversing continues until you start to like the person pretty well. You might try providing someone your phone number after you feel confident in their ability to be trusted.

Remember that taking this step toward developing a relationship is a huge one, so it's best to be safe than sorry.

When it comes to phone numbers, exchanging them back and forth, preferably simultaneously, is the safest course of action because it puts neither party at a disadvantage. It truly isn't a big thing; you may tell the person that you're simply being cautious and they'll understand. If he or she doesn't, there's a significant possibility that they won't comprehend a lot of other things either. In that case, let them go.

STEP 4 : FACE-TO-FACE INTERACTION

There is no reason to put off a face-to-face encounter once you have begun speaking on the phone because the relationship has already taken flight. So why do we still wait?

Wait; there's no need to pressure it. You shouldn't come across as overly eager to meet this person.

Allow several phone conversations to pass before deciding to meet. Additionally, there are a few things you should consider before your actual meeting.

The Meeting

It is not advisable to extend an invitation to someone's home before getting to know them well. You'd better pick a public area, ideally one with a large population, just in case, you know.

Because of this, most couples choose to meet for lunch or dinner in a restaurant. There is one benefit to sharing meals. When individuals eat and drink together, they learn a lot about one another.

You can learn a lot about a person by watching them eat, and table manners reveal a lot about a person's upbringing and culture. The second is that eating warm food has a tremendous impact on one's mental state. The tongue starts to wag and all those digestive juices come out.

Particularly after a few drinks of wine, people tend to loosen up considerably.

The first error that most individuals commit is believing—falsely—that any meeting, not even the first one, has to end with a trip to bed. No, that is not required.

You are not required to bring the individual home with you, either by you or anyone else. Simply because you enjoy chatting or conversing with someone does not obligate you to have a sexual relationship with them. Keep any such circumstances that might result in a bed room scene fully at away, and let that develop as well.

What is the procedure for doing that? Making sure the time is clear should be your first priority. Meetings might be challenging in the evenings. If you eat supper with someone, you can decide to drive them home afterward.

Of course, you can't just accept a ride and leave after getting dropped off without opening the door for the other person. And as a result of one thing leading to another, the inevitable will eventually occur. Naturally, if that's how you want things to be, you must follow my advice and refrain from doing what I just instructed you not to do.

Because most of us are at work throughout the day and can only set off an hour or so for lunch, lunchtime is the optimal time. As a result, you can always depart on the grounds that you need to return to work or something similar. After lunch, very few individuals really return home together. Another point is that romance does not significantly factor into lunchtime interactions.

Do your best to be to the designated location on time; you do not want to make a new acquaintance wait. Keep your style simple and appropriate for the situation, while also choosing clothes that flatter your figure.

Affirming Your Legacy

Suppose, though, that everything went according to plan and you both truly enjoyed each other's company. In such case, wouldn't you want the other person to think about and remember you? What steps can you take to ensure that the other person does consider you?

Simple is the response. Simply leave your mark. A business card or visitor's card is not acceptable in this situation, mind you. The painting gains a highly formal color as a result. You don't want the person to remember you only for your title or your credentials, after all. A more individualized solution would be preferable.

Put all of your artistic and creative abilities to use. You may write a few lyrical lines on a tiny card and give it to the person if you're gifted in that area. You should keep in mind that the phrases shouldn't be about the person specifically, but rather about universal themes like friendship, relationships, togetherness, warmth, or meetings. But write ahead of time and save it for when the time is appropriate. Never attempt to compose a poem on a paper napkin while the person in front of you is seated!

If you can't write poetry, you might be able to copy down some lines from someone else's poem and paste them on a card while acknowledging that the lines are not your own.

Hold onto such a token and wait for the appropriate occasion. Just before you leave, if you are certain that "this is the one," deliver it to the recipient while saying tremulously, "I made this for you." It is far preferable to say "I made this for you" rather than "I bought this for you," I assure you.

What happens, therefore, if you're not entirely certain that you want to see this individual again? Therefore, keep it close to you and reserve it for the following individual.

If the recipient is the correct person and you did give them this particular gift, they are certain to have a lot better impression of you.

Clothing Creates a Man (Or Woman)

When you go out to lunch, you do not need to be dressed to kill. The best part about lunch dates is that we would typically be wearing our work clothes, saving us the anguish of picking the appropriate attire for a first date.

Making your first date a group activity, ideally a foursome, is a lovely thing you could do. This eliminates the awkwardness of the circumstance and definitely eliminates all those awkward silences.

Another benefit of working in a group is that less attention will be paid to individual members, which reduces stress and makes both parties more at ease. Additionally, it is safer because there is safety in numbers.

However, the inclusion of the company should be voluntary and not imposed on the other party. The enjoyment is lost if one person dominates the conversation, so be careful to avoid somebody you know to be a chatterbox.

If you choose to, you may drink, but on your first date, don't indulge too much. Not only is it in poor taste, but being inebriated increases the likelihood that you may say something without meaning to and it might completely spoil the situation.

Paying for It

It is a good idea to decide in advance and let everyone know that you intend to go Dutch, which means that everyone will be responsible for paying for their own possessions. That is how it should be since you do not want to be held responsible for the individual if this relationship does not work out.

When selecting the location, stay away from remote areas and unfamiliar locations. But the environment is crucial. You can't expect to have a face-to-face conversation in a busy mall, can you? That pretty much sums up your first date, in my opinion.

Several Dates

What happens then if you receive multiple offers to date at nearly the same time?

Or, to put it another way, what happens if you develop intimate relationships with multiple people at once? Hey, that's probably exactly what we're searching for. You may go on several dates, then evaluate each one for yourself to determine who is the best match.

You are not required to jump for the first person who grabs your attention. You have the freedom to decide, so exercise it. As long as you don't tell somebody that you're seeing anyone else, there's no need to feel bad about two-timing them.

What would happen if date number one and date number 2 ended up at the same place at the same time? All you have to do is approach it naturally, as if nothing unusual is happening. Introduce dates No. 1 and 2 as your pals, then see how they interact. This is a great strategy to predict future jealous behavior from a spouse or wife.

A double date, or going out with two individuals at once, is entirely out of the question, though!

Making a good impression when dating offline

There are several things to your favor when you date online. For instance, you do not really need to worry about appearances because the other person cannot see you. You can focus all of your efforts on sounding witty and intelligent.

However, there are a myriad of factors to pay attention to when you are really seated in front of a person. Many people have the opinion that maintaining looks is not particularly important. They believe that being oneself is more crucial.

It has a passable sound. However, you must maintain your appearance, at least on your first date. You should make every effort to avoid such blunder because the other person shouldn't feel embarrassed to be seen out and about with you.

Let's begin by discussing your appearance. Even though I just said that you don't have to dress to kill, it's crucial that you seem well-groomed.

Pay close attention to your teeth, hair, and nails. Since having poor breath is the biggest turnoff, be sure to check it as well.

You shouldn't dress in a loud way that draws unwanted attention. Select clothing that fits you well while also making you feel comfortable.

Ladies, please use caution when applying makeup and keep in mind that it should enhance rather than conceal your appearance. It is better to stay away from loud colors.

Of course, you should smell good, but don't go overboard. We don't want the other person to remember you only for that one overwhelming smell. Men, please be careful to choose odors that are more masculine, like musk, or scents from nature. Keep it as light and elegant as you can, ladies.

Charm is the Key

The topics covered up to this point have all dealt with how to make a good impression. Making the other person feel at ease is something that is equally crucial, if not more so, than that. Aid the other person in relaxing.

In any case You two have been conversing for a while now, so you are well acquainted. You should try to reduce the tension and establish a friendly rapport.

The ice can occasionally become so thick that you can really feel it. Make a few jokes to break the ice.

But in order for the joke to work, it must be spontaneous and appropriate for the circumstance. Avoid practicing jokes because they tend to seem, well, practiced.

Charm is the essential word here. Put all of your charm to good use. Make an effort to be as considerate and thoughtful as you can. Instead of taking over the conversation, encourage the other person to speak. Asking about the other person's work can help you start a conversation because people typically enjoy talking about themselves. Show consideration for what the other person has to say.

Be as conversational as you can. A good conversationalist is someone who listens well in addition to talking well. So make an effort to pay attention. Additionally, avoid multitasking while you're listening to avoid giving the other person the impression that you're not interested in what they have to say.

What do you do if you see that the other person is monopolizing the discourse, then?

In that scenario, calmly listen for a minute or two before making a quiet gesture, like raising an eyebrow or smiling through the corner of your mouth. If the other person is smart enough, they will recognize the cue. Take a chance if you don't want to be forced to listen to this person for the rest of your life.

Humor typically works. But once more, be careful not to overdo it. Too much comedy is the only thing that might possibly be worse than a complete lack of humor.

Gifts?

It is a good idea to bring a present because it makes a nice first impression, but keep in mind that when you are courting, your gifts should only be flowers or chocolates. Try to learn what the other person enjoys in terms of flowers and chocolates while you are conversing. Giving someone who is allergic to flowers is definitely not a good idea.

The goal of your present should be to leave a positive and long-lasting impression rather than to win over the recipient. Spending a lot on a first date is pointless because there is no law stating that everything must go smoothly the first time. Don't go overboard while maintaining a professional appearance.

However, if the other person forgets to bring you a gift, be sure to quickly reassure them that everything will be fine. Keep the other person from feeling uncomfortable. That is a great way to lighten the conversation, in fact. You can lightheartedly request a gift from the other person the following time.

STEP 5 : ONCE BITTEN

What would they do if, as many of my readers may be concerned, nothing turns out exactly as was predicted? Alternatively, what should they do if their first date is unsuccessful?

Repeating the entire process again is the simple solution.

Retrace our steps and begin at the beginning. We may need to develop several plants before we receive the desired harvest, but keep in mind that this is your chance to select a spouse for life.

This is not a two-timing discussion. I'm saying to keep your options open rather than putting all your eggs in one basket. Do not rely solely on one individual since you run the risk of losing heart if it fails. The greatest is always possible, but you should also be prepared for the worst.

The right pick at the first attempt is only given to the truly lucky. We simply have to keep trying until we succeed, for the rest of us. You have the freedom to chose, which is an additional benefit of meeting new individuals. You shouldn't immediately fall head over heels for the first man or woman who crosses your path. Make the appropriate choice after giving yourself time and breathing room.

You can't be compelled to sign a contract by anyone. Your choice alone should determine it.

Of course, if you pick up on the proper cues and a part of you knows this is the right person for you, what are you waiting for? Give the go-ahead and give the green light.

However, if you feel pressured into making a commitment by someone else and you feel like you are being pushed, attempt to gently distance yourself from them. It's simply a matter of telling the person you need more time while putting your foot down very forcefully.

To keep someone waiting for too long, though, is not a smart idea. Describe your needs as maybe requiring a week or more of their time. However, keep the fact that you are examining other people a secret from the subject. Just let them know that you want to be sure because this is perhaps the most significant choice you will ever make.

A Final Word

Let me say one last thing before we say goodbye. Please be careful to go politely if things do not work out. Choosing to express such things over chat under such circumstances is not the wisest course of action. It's possible that the other person will ask you some extremely awkward questions that you won't know how to respond to.

The best course of action is to email the person and explain that while you had other plans for them, you still wanted to stay close friends.

The "good friends" component never fails, so you don't have to worry about the other person bugging you in the future. Most people find it offensive to be referred to be a good friend following a close encounter. Usually, this is followed by the relationship simply fizzling away. But kindly keep in mind that it is impolite to leave without saying goodbye and to simply cease returning emails that lack any kind of information.

Because they don't want to hurt the other person, some people act in that manner. It is actually worst when people are so heartless.

This concludes the discussion. Now that you are fully informed, the decision-making process is at your disposal. Therefore, why not get out there and make your presence felt and return with the catch of a lifetime.

Since I believe we have looked everywhere, I have no doubts about how well-in-control your first date will be.

In order for you to have online dating success!

www.ingramcontent.com/pod-product-compliance
Lightning Source LLC
Chambersburg PA
CBHW070338120526
44590CB00017B/2928